Someday,
after we have mastered
the winds, the waves, the tides and gravity…,
we shall harness the energies of love.
Then,
for the second time in the history of the world,
man will have discovered fire.

– Teilhard de Chardin

Balboa Press books may be ordered through booksellers or by contacting:

Balboa Press
A Division of Hay House
1663 Liberty Drive
Bloomington, IN 47403
www.balboapress.com
1 (877) 407-4847

Print information available on the last page.

ISBN: 978-1-9822-2299-4 (sc)
ISBN: 978-1-9822-2301-4 (hc)
ISBN: 978-1-9822-2300-7 (e)

Library of Congress Control Number: 2019902392

Balboa Press rev. date: 07/12/2019

PRAYERS FOR A NEW MILLENNIUM

a collection of poems and musings

Rodolfo León

BALBOA
PRESS

A DIVISION OF HAY HOUSE

Contents

Author's Note

This collection of poems and musings (except for fifteen of them) was originally completed in the spring of 1999, and then I had a disabling bicycle accident in the fall of that year. As a result of becoming disabled, I found myself in an ideal situation to think about and write the kind of book I had wanted to read since I was in high school, a book that would explain the meaning of life in a simple, reasonable, and satisfying way. I used many of these poems in that book to illustrate my explanations of the meaning of life. Feel free to write to me at my e-mail address (dleon19@atlanticbb. net) or at my backup e-mail address (dleon1919@yahoo.com) to request that I send you the PDF of that book about the meaning of life, *Unity in Diversity: a new dawn,* which explains the reasoning behind many of these poems. Also, feel free to write to me if you would like an explanation of any of these poems, or for any other reason. I love to communicate with my readers. And although my real name is Rodolfo, I go by David, so feel free to call me David.

Acknowledgments

I would like to thank Cristina, Elena, Barbara, and Marcin (especially Barbara and Marcin) for their unique influences on the creation of this collection of poems and musings. I would also like to express a special gratitude to the people of João Pessõa (Brazil) and Cloud Mountain Retreat Center (Washington, USA), where the majority of these poems and musings were written.

Preface

The majority of these poems were written over a fourteen-month period. I met a woman with whom I became infatuated, and I found myself composing poems for her. Then I began writing poems about other stuff that was weighing on me. I never intended to become a poet, but in just over a year, I had written over fifty poems.

A friend urged me to seek publication, but she was a very, very good friend (with much in common), so I did not take her praise too seriously. However, as a result of her appreciation, I began sharing my poems with others. Eventually, the momentum of positive feedback convinced me that they deserved to be shared more broadly.

During the same period that I was seriously asking myself whether these poems deserved to be published, I had this strange and powerful dream.

> I was on the back porch (actually, a screened patio) of my grandparents' old house (the one where I'd spent all my most memorable Christmases) with my grandfather, with whom I had always had a unique

connection (and who had died of cancer a few years prior to when I began writing these poems). We were alone, talking privately and openly in the manner that we always had.

There were people in the house, family members lurking busily behind the thick curtains and sliding glass doors that opened onto the patio. He was very sick; we both knew that he didn't have much time. "I don't want to die in a hospital," he said. "I want to stop all of these sickening treatments and die in peace. Please don't let them take me. Can you do that?"

My family meant well, but for all their supposed faith in God and an afterlife, I could not comprehend how they could behave so fearfully and desperately in the face of my grandfather's impending death. I told him that I would. I told him not to worry, that I would take care of everything. He seemed to relax.

We stood staring through the screen that surrounded the patio out at the backyard together. He asked me about my life. I wasn't so young anymore. Did I want to have children? What was to become of the family name? My grandfather had immigrated to the United States in his forties, fleeing a homeland in the throes of a communist revolution. He had lost almost everything, and like so many others of his kind, what he valued most in this new country was his family.

I explained that I did not feel called to have children. I wanted to dedicate myself to writing, and being able to share in this way with others was what moved me.

He listened patiently and nodded as if he understood. And then, in an offhand manner, he began to ask me about one of my cousins who was studying to become a doctor, about how we got along. I told him that all his grandchildren, of whom I was the oldest, got along fine, and everyone was fine.

Suddenly, a large fishing spool, the kind I used to fish with at canals in my youth, fell to the grass at our feet just beyond the screen. I looked up and saw that the thick nylon line from the spool led to a balloon floating in the sky. Before I knew it, my grandfather had magically stepped through the screen and straddled the line in the yard. As soon as it was between his legs, up he went. I pressed my face to the screen to get a better look. He was rising quickly to the balloon, and when he reached it, it popped, and both he and the balloon disappeared. I ran through the door of the patio out into the yard to get a better look. The yard had become full of things that had fallen from the sky. The sky was empty but for many small pieces of crumpled paper that were catching the bright sunlight as they fell to the grass. I was crying.

He's gone, I thought, displaying an emotionalism that was absent in my waking life. *My grandfather is out of my life forever.*

I scanned the ground and saw that it was littered with common items my grandfather had used daily: bowls and silverware, pens and keys, his wallet... And all these bits of crumpled paper.

I picked one of them up and opened it. There, written in my own script, were some lines that I had used in a poem. I began opening some other pieces of the bits of crumpled paper. They all contained notes in my handwriting; they were all rough drafts of verses I had formed into poems. With that realization, I awoke.

I don't know where poems come from, or why some move us and some don't, or why certain things that can't be explained make sense to us and others that can, don't. I don't know if these poems are a gift from my grandfather, or if they'll help you as they've helped me, or if poems or dreams mean much in the end. There are questions in our lives that seek answers no one can give us.

If these poems speak to you, it is for you alone to search yourself to learn why.

Rodolfo León
Miami, Florida
Spring 1999

The Poems and Musings

Falling

When the wind blows hard without a care
And thoughts of you get in my hair,
My flowers sing their songs of sun
And new dreams grow where there were none.
And all my needs seem less and less
As fear gives way to endlessness.
I find no world to hunger for.
The lights that led can blind no more.
When eternity calls from a stranger's face,
The wind beats hard in a silent place.

To Scratch with Words

Not quite right behind my ear,
Not quite just beneath my heart,
At the root of every tear,
Where my deepest feelings start,
A tiny place that calls to me,
Whose song upon the air is such
As if it begs lost love from me…
But it's too close for me to touch.
My cares I send like magic birds
To reach the only way I know
This little itch, and scratch with words
In places fingers cannot go.

Feeling Is First

Feeling is first.
And when it comes to what's called love
And feeling your heart burst,
You're magically guided from above.

Romeo and Juliet,
From the moment they first met,
Felt that thing so deep and tender
That's now a lesson for all to remember.

Thoughts are fine
And keep us in line.
But if we want our hearts to burst,
Remember this truth: feeling is first.

Convenience

Lying still within the grass,
I hear them clearly as they pass.
Rubber on smooth asphalt yields
Speed and ease up mounds, past fields.
Like my pulse, they seem to bear
My blood, but few must be aware:
These dragons take their life from me,
And those inside pretend they're free
As dragons' breath kills us slowly.
Who could their senseless mother be?

Monsters

Don't trust the world; don't trust yourself.
Keep open things closed; guard like wealth.
Store your love safe deep within;
Protect it from each passing sin.
The days will rob, the years will steal,
Unless you hope from life conceal.
And wreaking pain and breeding hate,
Will drain you till it's much too late.

By living thus you'll have preserved
A place to store your heart, conserved.
But when you look out from life's crest,
The things you see won't bring you rest.
Don't look far for monsters there;
Look here within the breast you wear.
Imagined far-off monsters scare.
Real monsters here are everywhere.

Walking on the Beach, Like Waves

Walking on the beach while young,
My skin made brown from so much sun,
I kicked the waves and walked the sands,
The warmth of summer in my hands.

But now I walk the beach anew.
My steps are slow; my thoughts are too.
And smile for that child I once was,
Removed by time (as time so does)
And wonder at this motion still,
Of waves and sand and life's lone will.

How could I have outrun the tides,
Exceed my source with all my strides?
But they have not forgotten me.
I'll too, like waves, return to sea.

Not Bread Alone

Man cannot live by bread alone,
Nor beds nor barns nor beauty.
So I searched far, where hunger shone,
As if from some lost duty.

Curiosity confronting fear
Can lead one to great heights,
Far within a bigger here
On deep and lonely nights.

And frightening as that may feel,
I fear far more compliance
For comfort cannot hunger steal,
Nor least compare, like silence.

Voices

It hurts to feel for someone who
Says they'll call but never do.
How to know this thing on fire
Is pure and true or just desire?
Wild, strong feelings fascinate,
But wishful thoughts don't satiate.
Thanks for moments sweet and free
You were kind to share with me.
Another time, and much less fuss…
Things might have been different for us.

It takes a fool to court a fall:
Ignore the writing on the wall.
Live your life; seek your own sun;
Don't look or lean towards anyone.
Forget the who, the where, the why,
And come and go of years gone by.
Take care of you; let others be.
Fate will touch each differently.
And when time ends, when life's departed,
You'll find yourself back where you started.

Why is it that this hunger vents
If not from some sure sustenance
That, coming first, prepares the ground
For wondrous things to grow unbound?
To live a loner's life I would
If in my heart I felt I should.
To live a joy that's sure to end
Is something minds can't comprehend.
I ask just this: Is this just me
Or something more that's meant to be?

A Kiss

just   a kiss
just   a light   kiss
just an I know what it's like kiss
just to know what it's like to kiss
when the night wets your smile like a kiss
and the warmth in my eyes would not miss
we could lean close and touch with our lips
it would just be a kiss
just a kiss

Some Things Only Fate Can Do

Some things only fate can do.
If you love him, but I love you,
I turn around and walk away;
Let fate do what all fate may.
For in this place of dreams and ground,
Not just worlds go round and round.
I'll maybe one day turn to find
You in my life again, inclined
This time to take what's yours in me,
And do those things meant just for two,
And help to build for us a we,
And give to me what's mine in you.

Searching

Searching for holy words to touch my soul,
I wandered far and high on lonely hills.
Ignoring earthly needs to reach my goal,
I sailed cold winds but never felt their chills.

And crossing all the pain that I could bear,
As if with it to tear what's not from me,
I lost my way, and words that I would share
Dried up and left me lying nakedly.

Why had my life led me to some dark hole?
Feeling too frail to know something so free,
How could I now expect to touch my soul?
Just then, at last, I felt my soul touch me.

If I Could Live Again

If I could live again,
I'd want to live it all.
I wouldn't stir or strive when
Half-baked urges came to call.
Fuck what everybody does.
Fuck the things done just to prove.
I wouldn't change how anybody was;
I'd learn to transform my own groove.

If I could live again,
I'd sail my dreams for gold.
I'd ride out all my hunches, then
I'd learn to live them bold.
I'd never go half wanting,
And I wouldn't go if shoved.
I'd seek only what was haunting
Me, and only things I loved.

Believe

"Believe," he'd said,
His body now dead.
His memory still dancing and burning in me,
And calling me past all my doubts to believe.

"Believe," he'd said,
"When I wore youth's head,
We used a real icebox and radio was new.
We thought we had done all our efforts could do."

"Believe," he'd said.
The faith that he fed
Now rises up in me and carries me on,
Even as I distress that my grandfather's gone.

"Believe," I hear,
His song in my tears,
"The things you'll see change, you can barely conceive.
Life will overmake you. Believe, son, believe."

Are You a (Religion)?

Say in response to that foolish old question:
"Only as much as Christ was a Christian,
And only as much as Buddha a Buddhist,
Or Mohammed a Muslim, or Lao Tzu a Taoist."
It's clear that they never worshipped and waited.
Seek truth for yourself, just as all they did.

Graduation Day

(My parents asked me to write a poem for my sister in honor of her high school graduation to be published in her high school yearbook next to some photos of her. This is what I wrote. The shock expressed in the first line of this poem is due to the fact that my mother unexpectedly became pregnant with my sister when she was thirty-six years old – it was a completely unplanned pregnancy.)

"Dear God, a child! What are we to do?"
You will fill it with love as your parents filled you.
"Dear God, but what if it isn't like us?"
You will bridge every difference with respect and trust.
"But God, can we do as You ask us to do?"
If you love as I love, it will carry you through.

Parents must provide what their children might lack,
And they do never knowing what it is they'll get back.
For God in God's wisdom would have it this way:
That while parents worry, their children can play.
And then they grow up and do as they may.
It's hard to let go on graduation day.

"See these pictures, dear God, of the dream child you gave?
She is real – now a woman – self-guided and brave!
See her walk, see her turn, see her laugh and smile.
We have done all we could, every day, every mile.
Of ourselves we have given as You said that we should.
But You made it too easy. This child was too good."

May the love that we've fed you carry you on,
Regardless of distance and after we're gone.
May it guide and protect you and make bright your way,
And banish the doubts that cause others to stray.
And may faith lead you toward what for you shall be true,
Just as it had led us to the treasure of you.

Warm Light

Warm light poured down to kiss my face...
I've never felt more of God's grace
Than in those moments, standing there,
Feeling more love than I could bear.

This light was so alive in me,
I wore it plain for all to see.
I'd grab my fellows by their arms
To share with them its sensuous charms.

But they were busy. I could see
They saw but lived on lifelessly.
I asked in wonder at my care:
Is this not something I can share?

But they'd built windows, they'd built walls
To catch the light from where it falls
And feed it to their hearts in bits,
But hearts so starved had turned to pits.

To live among a lifeless throng
Is sad; sometimes I think it's wrong
With all this light – so bright, so free –
To live enclosed, afraid, darkly.

But what else can a poet do
But join the light and shine bright too?
If they can't drink light poured so free,
Perhaps they'll take its fruit from me.

Lullaby

Now I lay me down to sleep
To commune with what is deep.
Far beyond my thoughts I go
To a place I cannot know.
In sleep there is no consciousness,
Where thought divides and separates.
In sleep we drink of oneness,
And oneness is what satiates.

To Reach a Friend

If I built a bridge to you,
Would you build a bridge to me?
Past time and space, just for two,
A bridge across infinity.
Across the lives that we have led,
Across the tears that we have shed,
Across the things we'll never tell,
Across whatever private hell,
Across the trials that fate may send;
Across, with hope, to reach a friend.

But bridges burn and bridges rot.
Bridges across infinity cannot
Unite whatever love we share
For too long or with much care.
For just as life gives time to play,
Life, in time, takes all away
But that ocean and that ground
Where our souls embrace unbound.

So let our bridges burn and fall.
Try to save them not at all.
Let life take them all away.
Dreams to dust is what we pay.
Leaving what is deep to bear
All the love that we would share.
And when our hearts rest in that place,
In that vast eternal space,
No need to bind, no need to pair,
Dust sprung from love that's everywhere.

Different

You have your pretty car, your pretty life, your pretty kids.
On Sunday, you wake late then go to church and talk your dids.
On Monday, you wake early, go to work until it's late.
On Friday, you eat out or stay at home to contemplate.

And one day you'll rise more slowly.
And one day you'll rise no more.
And one day you'll find yourself alone,
Alone upon death's door.

Then maybe you'll remember all those others you once knew,
Those who with you woke to go to work or go to school.
Those upon the wayside, those on higher walks,
Those of different color, different cares, or different talks.

And when you rise more slowly,
And when you rise no more,
And when you find yourself alone,
Alone upon death's door,

Those others you thought different, unfamiliar, or untaught,
Those others you would hate for taking things your blood had bought,
Those others you would envy or resent for having more,
They'll all be standing naked next to you upon death's door.

And then you'll smile more slowly.
And then you'll cry no more.
And then you'll know you're not alone,
Alone upon death's door.

For all our trials seem different to us each within this life,
And hard earned is the wisdom that would see past our own strife.
But one day we shall face this simple truth and nothing more:
Our shadows are the same, for all the same, upon death's door.

At Last

I've walked these roads so many times before,
But never like today.
It's never been so clear to me
That now I'm going away.
Maybe it was those gray hairs
Or sexual apathy.
I watch others striving hard for things
That I no longer see.
Someone wants a bigger house
Or buys a brand-new car.
To me the roads all seem the same,
But now home feels so far.
My bed's too small to comfort me.
My family's not my own.
And little quiet moments now
Can chill me to the bone.
Something here I don't yet see;
I've been blind for so long.
This feeling swallows everything.
I tell myself, "Be strong."

Faith is what I travel now,
Not roads or streets or walks.
And unknown voices in my depths
Surprise me with their talks:
"Every single breath you take
You give back in the end.
People you'd thought strangers,
Through death's eyes, you see as friends."

Was I just a season?
Was I ever young or free?
Or were those just sensations felt
By what I felt was me?

It's too much for my head now;
It all appears a lie.
Nobody'd ever told me this
Is what it's like to die.
"You give back every breath you take,
And everything that's you
Stays here; it does not carry on.
There's nothing you can do."

At first it seemed so terrible and sad,
This simple fact.
Was there after all no God
With whom I'd made a pact?
I'd lived an honest, humble life,
And now I seemed so caught
Within the grip of time, alone,
And left, alone, to rot.
But silence has a fullness now.
I don't feel so alone.
I'm finding some far deeper warmth
Beyond the chill of bone.
Maybe there is not a God
Awaiting me above.
But now that I know all is lost,
At last, I'm free to love.

Not Enough

It's not enough that I love you
And that I know you love me too.
It's not enough that late at night,
You're near to hold and hold me tight.
It's not enough that when I cry,
You understand and don't ask why.
It's not enough that life with you
Means so much more than all I do.

For even deep within your arms
I feel the sound of soft alarms.
Of things I know I need to face
Alone beyond your warm embrace.
Of clawing doubts and troubling thoughts,
Inviting to untie their knots,
And do the things I have to do
To bring me closer to what's true.

It's not something I lack from you
Or that the joys we share are few.
But how can I love boundlessly
Unless I've vanquished fear from me?
I need to go into this doubt
To let whatever haunts me out.
Until I've crossed this pain and strife,
I'll never feel at home in life.

Freedom from Choice

If freedom unites
But choices exclude,
Where does that leave
Freedom to choose?
To choose what we want
Divides what is whole,
Yet binding these parts
Is freedom's great role.

A senseless dance,
It seems to me,
To choose and divide,
Then let flow and be free
Just to choose once again
To increasing degree,
On and on without end
So ridiculously.

Desire to extend
What we think we must be
Is what we must end
To live peacefully.
Desire to choose –
Even choose to be free –
Is what we must lose
To be free endlessly.

Taking to the High(er) Way

When I was young, they used to say,
"Live your dreams. Don't let them stray."
Until they learned my dreams weren't theirs,
That I didn't care for cars or furs.

The comforts they would have me choose
Would forgo truths I would not lose.
From common needs I sought release
To amplify my sense of peace.

"But then what will you do for money?
We just want what's best for you, honey."
But I hungered for things much more basic to live,
Things I soon learned all their caring couldn't give.

Money or not, we were all going to die.
What I needed most was a reason to try:
Something bigger than life to carry me on
And take me past death in an infinite dawn.

"I have to do this in my own unique way.
Whatever the pain, that's the price I'll pay.
And live my questions out to their end,
And hope that there, they'll answers lend."

Some say I'm crazy, but I say it's them,
Who prize a doomed life like some precious gem.
It's true I don't know what I will meet,
But that beats living a dead-end street.

Twenty-First Century Mantra

A million years we walked afraid
To touch with hands that love has made:
Love's heart put deep inside our soul,
As if within an endless hole.

Afraid to bridge eternity,
We moved along ever slowly,
With hope our only guiding light
To spur us on our inner flight.

Faith in the rain, faith in the sun,
Faith in the plants and beasts we'd won,
Searching for what to call our own...
But each step left us more alone.

We've worshipped kings, God's sons on Earth;
We've worshipped things imbued with worth.
We've fought for bragging rights to God,
Then rights to Earth once that felt odd.

Through all the years, our sense has grown
That nothing we can call our own.
But open hearts and granted trust
Can build a heaven out of dust.

Now is the time; we hear love calling
What is ours in each of us.
The time has come; this is the dawning
Of the age of Aquarius.

Of All That Hurts

Of all that hurts that I can find,
Nothing compares to this, simply:
To fit my soul within my mind
Is all that's really killing me.

To rip my feelings into words
And act from fear of losing love,
To live among untrusting herds
Ignoring callings from above,
Is more than my soft heart can bear –
Is worse than any other pain –
And leaves me much too numb to care.
Such normalcy cannot be sane.

But what else is this world about?
What else can a person do?
These sorts of things my mind cries out.
These sorts of things and others too.

I understand one thing for sure:
To live the life my mind conceives
Is not so grand nor sweet nor pure –
Cannot compare in any way
To all these depths my soul believes –
And damn to hell what thoughts may say.

Destiny

Trees rise high up from the grass.
Birds fly whistling as they pass.
And little critters in the ground,
And skies and lakes and all around.

Even clouds know where to go,
And shifting winds from whence they blow,
And planets floating far away
Spin on in their own magic way.

All these things all have their place
And dance with their own private grace
Without question, doubt, or fear
As to how or why they're here.

And so, too, our human race
Must flow within designs of grace
And live out its humanity:
That each of us traverse our "me".

Sailing to India

The world was flat, and now it's round.
Our feet still walk on solid ground.
Or so we think, just like we thought
The world was flat, but know it's not.

Six hundred years ago, our shell
Was one side Heaven, one side Hell.
Now we have a spinning sphere
And galaxies both far and near.

But life is still unclear to us.
"A certain end seems obvious,"
They say. "Just like a world that's flat,
Our lives have ends; that will be that."

Yet even then, all those years back,
There were some who didn't lack
Vision to see the world as round
And raise their senses from the ground.

So now we hear wise people say,
"Life's end only appears that way.
Just like worlds aren't flat, but whole,
There is no death – just endless soul."

But many people still don't see
Beyond what old traditions decree.
Too snug to question what they dread,
They'd rather live enclosed, half dead.

It's not for me to change their minds.
I follow the path my passion winds,
Moving on freely with deep faith that
Senses through love our being's not flat.

A Poet's Job

Putting into words what hurts
Is what a poet's meant to do.
Broken glass and bloodied shirts
Must be traversed to speak what's true.

Vocabulary's not enough,
And clever rhymes will bore and tire.
A poet needs much finer stuff
To capture inspiration's fire.

A brave heart unconfused by tears
To travel deep where feelings grow,
And pass through pain and rage and fears
To where love and love's passions flow.

That won't turn from emotions which
Disturb, repulse, or terrify.
A poet fits feelings so rich
Into swift thoughts so they won't die.

Patience is required too.
And silence, unseen like a ghost,
To still what needs to be pierced through
Then clearly grasp what hides from most.

And vision that sees past what seems
So real to eyes fixed on today
To bring to light those future dreams
For which our hearts silently pray.

But what is needed most is soul,
A soul well traveled through and through,
For poets to fulfill their role
And show what's in us all to you.

A New Dawn

Silent rain on silent seeds
Is waking up once-silent needs.
In each of us, deep in our hearts,
Is where the silent growing starts.

When we have had enough of things,
A deeper yearning in us stings.
And as our pain moves tears to flow,
This very rain makes new things grow.

Out of the ground where we'd felt lost,
Among the hopes that we had tossed,
Where old roots wind a worn-out course,
New growths reach out from some new source.

Then slowly we begin to feel,
As leaves turned toward the sky implore,
A sun is shining now for real
That we had only dreamt before.

Jesus Says

Jesus says that it's okay
For me to turn my eyes away
From all the things that I've been told
That I should want and gain and hold.

Jesus says there's nothing good
In life's great urge that says I should
Want and need and build and make
So many things for my own sake.

Jesus says that there is joy
Beyond this life if I employ
A deeper faith in things beyond
This life's delights, however fond.

For one day I'll die anyway,
No matter what I do or pray.
And if that day should be today,
Jesus says that that's okay.

Open Your Heart

Open your heart just this wide:
Remove your vanity and pride.
God will melt away your fears
And all the weight of passing years.

Open your heart even more:
Remove those needs within your core.
God will sing into your ears
Till all the darkness disappears.

Throw away your heart for good:
Just leave faith where love once stood.
God will let you roam freely
The whole of all eternity.

Only Faith

First faith is a mist,
And you breathe it.
Then it rains and forms rivers and lakes,
And you swim in it.
Then the lakes freeze and form ice,
And you walk on it.
Then the ice cracks and swallows you,
Leaving
Only faith.

Dear Sun

You're so pretty in the sky;
No brighter, richer love I've found.
And I have looked; you know I've tried.
I've searched far and high this ground.

And I am not the only one
Who turns to you so reverently.
So many creatures worship sun
To bathe in warmth more nakedly.

Dear sun, I've got a problem here.
You see these paths that man has made?
I've tried them all – plain, without fear –
Searching in them for what I've craved.

But none fulfills me; none sustains.
Nor motivates me to renew
This urge to share deep in my veins
That you, above all else, imbue.

The only one that calls is you –
Your light, your heat, your openness.
But my life is yet far from through,
And I'm not moved to make it less.

I've just one question, if you please.
Let's say I set my sights past man.
Let's say I start to live like trees,
Reaching towards you all that I can.

Would you tell me what to do
With all these years that aren't yet through,
Make sure they're lived pure and true,
If I surrender them to you?

Stand

I tried to walk my parents' road,
Thinking they'd know what's best for me,
But could not justify the load
Nor do things I did not believe.

I walked my generation's road,
Thinking it'd be what's best for me,
Until discovering that their load
Was but a masked conformity.

I took an independent road,
Thinking I'd sense what's best for me,
And followed intuition's load
Beyond accepted sanity.

I found myself upon a road,
A quiet road that carried me,
Unburdened me of all my load
And all my thoughts of what should be.

I realize now my life's a road,
A road upon an inner land,
That cannot predefine its load,
And where it goes is where I stand.

I Know Why

I know why we worship death
And keep God in a word so small,
As if our lives began in breath
And not something bigger than all.

I know why to live our heart
Is something we can't do gladly.
Because the heart would have us start,
And nothing more, incessantly.

And I know why silence is worse
Than strain and hurt and loss and pain.
It undermines our blessed curse
And blows away like dust all gain.

Truth is such a deadly grace.
It swallows you up into me
And then consumes both time and space
Leaving, instead, eternity.

I Know Why (Explained)

(For those who would like to know what I mean with this poem.)

> I know why we worship death
> And keep God in a word so small,
> As if our lives began in breath
> And not something bigger than all.

(What I mean with "we worship death" is simply that we believe that we are going to die, and what I mean with "keep God in a word so small" is simply that we have very limited beliefs about what God is, like the belief that God is an old man in the sky who judges us. And the last two lines above simply express that we believe our lives begin when our physical bodies are born, and not when our souls are created by God, or whatever you want to call the force that creates our souls.)

> I know why to live our heart
> Is something we can't do gladly.
> Because the heart would have us start,
> And nothing more, incessantly.

(What I mean with the stanza above is that our heart wants us to live in the moment, in the present, and nothing more, on and on. But we cannot do that happily because our minds are always concerned with the past and the future.)

And I know why silence is worse
Than strain and hurt and loss and pain.
It undermines our blessed curse
And blows away like dust all gain.

(What I mean with the stanza above is that silence, specifically stopping our mental chatter and listening to our soul, which speaks to us through the silence that is beyond our mental chatter, is worse than the terrible things we experience from our egos, like strain and hurt and loss and pain, because it will destroy our egos. I express this by saying that it will undermine our blessed curse, our egos. And it will destroy the importance of the material world, which I express by saying that it will blow "away like dust all gain".)

Truth is such a deadly grace.
It swallows you up into me
And then consumes both time and space
Leaving, instead, eternity.

(What I mean with this last stanza is that truth, the truth of who we really are and the truth of what life is really about, is very deadly and destructive because truth will show us that we are all spiritually united, which I express by saying that truth "swallows you up into me", and truth will expose the lie of physical existence and make it clear to us that we are actually spiritual beings that live eternal lives. We live for an eternity, which I express by saying that truth "consumes both time and space", replacing them with eternity, which I express by saying "Leaving, instead, eternity". Basically, this poem is saying "I know why we avoid truth. It is because truth will tragically expose the lie of physical existence, destroy our faith in our physical being, and leave us our spiritual nature instead, which is eternal.")

The Real Crime

I don't think the birds will care
If they die of DDT
Or get eaten up somewhere
By bigger things that they can see.

And I don't think the whales will ask
Why it had to be this way.
A greedy beast, a greedy task:
They knew we'd come to kill one day.

And I don't think the Earth agrees
Or needs us here to travel space.
It's only us who thinks she needs
The presence of our human race.

"Death is death," some people say.
"How it's done's extraneous.
Birds, whales, man… all die one day.
Or we eat them, or they eat us."

Dying is a fact of life,
But death is but a fleeting end.
And those whose hopes lie with a knife,
From their own hell never ascend.

And Soul Remains

Like some great ocean that I swim,
There is a power that I reap:
Something eternal deep within
That I partake of when I sleep.

Nearer than my beating heart,
Closer than my silent pleas,
Lies in me this unseen part,
Because it is the thing that sees.

This ancient home beyond my mind,
From whence all of my callings drift –
Nor harsh nor sweet nor cruel nor kind –
Awaits the lie called me to lift.

Still and silent, patiently,
Watching all the things I do,
It swallows all that I call me,
And sole remains when me is through.

Existence Is Its Own

Existence
Is its own reason, power, miracle, motive.
Get out of its way.
It will fill all the empty places.

How Much Love

How much love
Do you need to pour
Into a person
Before that person
Becomes
A loving person?

Moving Mountains

To those who would move mountains,
Those who move with mountains
Appear to move those mountains.

Heaven by Default

Looking out from where I sit,
Wondering how long fear will fill
Our hearts… Will violence ever quit?
Will vanity remain our plan?
Feeding needs that suit blind will,
In greed we take all that we can.

Another reckless thousand years…
We'll soon begin to feel the chill
Of acting from unfounded fears,
And Earth will finally swallow man.
Many say it surely will,
And even those grab what they can.

But rising from this hopelessness,
A pain not even greed could kill
Drives us through hell, beyond darkness,
In search of what would transform man.
And love is the only thing that will.
Love is the only thing that can.

Unity in Diversity

Remembering Angie

(After our dog died in 2014, I felt moved to write this simple poem in her memory.)

Tiny steps and wagging tail
Greet me daily without fail
Every day when I get home,
Reminding me I'm not alone.

Only memories left for me;
Her wagging tail I'll no more see.
Crying, crying all day long
'Cause now my darling doggie's gone.

Thank you, Lord, for all those years.
Memories now console my tears.
Walks through parks and chasing doves,
Reminders of the things she loved.

All those things I did with her,
My precious angel dressed in fur.
Reminders of the love we share.
Memories ease the loss I bear.

Someone

I don't need a pretty face
To take with me to every place,
Nor someone who says I'm the one
They care for more than anyone,
Nor feelings linking so strongly
They'd last a whole eternity.
No, I don't need a person near
To help me face the things I fear.

And I don't want somebody who
Is fixed and thinks that I'm fixed too,
Nor hide within another's heart
From freedoms I alone must chart,
Nor pour my passion into things
To bind me as on puppet strings.
No, I don't want the kind of love
that would pull from the sky a dove.

But I could use a steady hand
To soothe me like rains soothe the land.
And bright eyes and bright smiles that say
The stars shine from the Earth each day.
And laughter warmer than the sun,
Enough to share with everyone.
Yes, I could use somebody who
Sees what's outside inside them too.

Equanimity

These worn, stiff hands are but quite new
Compared to what this heart's been through.
And all the many miles I've walked
Cannot compare to words I've talked.
And things I've heard and seen and done...
Except for age, you'd think I'd won
Some stately gain, some kingly game.
But bliss for me is much the same.

A simple walk breathing clean air,
A simple smile worn without care,
A simple silence to reflect
And muse upon, less circumspect...
These things that bring me peace and joy,
As much right now as when a boy,
Are all that's left of want in me.
I relish them and let life be.

I've learned some things I wouldn't have guessed
About how dreams can manifest:
About how feelings subtly show
One when to stop and when to go.
I know them with less strength to act,
But now that I can see through fact,
Life's vanity does not sway me.
Age grants this equanimity.

As It Should Be

Would you know what life's like free,
Unspoiled and wild, as it should be?
Not all tied up in nine to fives
Or trapped within stale people hives.

Would you know what it would do
If it were not so bound to you?
Without your fear, without your haste,
It would behave much less misplaced.

Treat it like its own willed thing.
Watch it roam and shit and sing.
Let it shed its clothes to play.
Listen as it turns to pray.

Don't confuse your love for it
With your fool need to make it fit.
Your whims and pride and loneliness
Are not what it prefers to dress.

Watch it like you would the sky.
Watch it swallow how and why.
In time it will to heaven grow.
Just set it free. Then you'll know.

Just This

We're not from another star,
But we have come from very far
To trace an image in this place,
With sweat and blood and tears, God's grace.
The power that has made us so
Beyond our needs drives us to grow
And teaches what we must unchoose
To strip away what we must lose
To realize where we are from
And then undo what we have done
To cloud the waters of this place
That have obscured from us God's face.

What's Coming

Life will squash you like a little bug
Or crush your fears upon the ground of love,
Will beat you slowly far into despair
Or gently spread your heart out everywhere,
Will blind you with bright light till your eyes sting
Or help you see yourself in everything.
The difference between bliss and agony
In all the things you hear and feel and see
Is to know the tune that life is humming
And accept with grace in you God's coming.

The Ultimate Truth

There is only one god.
Or rather,
There is only one: God.

Dawning

A word to make things different here?
I smile at things I used to fear,
At things no longer seen as true.
I know now what I have to do.

No matter how immense the thought,
What I've unlearned cannot be taught
In words that would just say I'm less
Than all I feel as beingness.

Let my steps more freely flow;
Watch imagination grow.
Don't pretend to clearly know
What is just and what is so.

More and more I feel so small
Learning to accept it all.
And when it doesn't accept me,
I set my preconceptions free.

In time I know that life gives way,
But I can act from that today,
Releasing what is spinning round
To feel in me a firmer ground.

What I am may be the same,
Though more than any given name,
Including all that I have seen
And all that will or's ever been.

As I wake from life's dull dreams,
History's not what it seems.
I sense I'm bathing in such light…
It flows from me. There is no night.

Do It Now

Every moment of every day,
Like a song in my head that won't go away,
I can hear my heart very clearly say,
"Do it now! Do it now!
Now's all you've got; do it now!"

Don't leave things until tomorrow
Because regret soon turns to sorrow.
And your heart will keep repeating
Every moment that it's beating,
"Do it now! Do it now!
Now's all you've got; do it now!"

Don't get mired in when, why, how.
Be brave enough to live in now.
And let these words become a vow:
"Do it now! Do it now!
Now's all you've got; do it now!"

One day, not long ago, we met.
And since then I've been trying to get
To know you better just to see
What these feelings for you might be.
I still don't know what to make of you;
I still don't know if what I feel is true.
But I know what my soul's urging me to do
Right now because my heart is telling me to
Do it now, and say, "I love you."

Yes, I love you. I love you.
And I know it's crazy because I barely know you.
But it feels good to express what I know to be true.

Every Face Tells a Story

(Watching people walk by from my wheelchair at a place called the Lincoln Road Mall in Miami Beach inspired me to write this poem.)

Every face tells a story:
Sad to be alive
Or living in glory;
Struggling to survive
Or living without worry;
Wanting to consume more and more and more,
Or moving through life eager to learn and explore.

Football is a game of inches.
Basketball's a game of angles.
Some faces say that their life pinches.
Some faces say that they are angels.

Do you prefer to live in fear
And wear a face without much cheer?
Or would you rather see through the gray
And wear your face a more cheerful way?
And not using your brain to its full capacity
Reflects on your face as a lack of curiosity.

Yes, every face tells a story:
Between feeling distraught about why you're here
And living peacefully without worry;
Between living in a constant state of fear
And living in a constant state of glory.

So what's your face say? What's your story?
Are you living in fear or living in glory?

Be Who You Are

(This poem is actually the lyrics to a song that came to me one night in April 2016. When I first published this book, I included a note here inviting anybody interested in helping me bring this song to life to contact me. Well, somebody did. A wonderful Mexican woman named Erika who purchased my books contacted me to say that she loved them. She is a video producer who has made some videos about me and my *World Without Walls* project and posted them on YouTube to help me attract more people to join my efforts to transform our world for the better. She also put me in contact with Yeye, her yoga teacher in Mexico, who is a singer. Together with her husband, Justin, who is a musician, Yeye helped me transform this poem into a wonderful song. I explained to them through Skype what the song sounded like in my head, and they came up with and recorded a version of this song that is even better than the one in my head. Please contact me if you would like me to send you the audio file of this song. My e-mail address appears in the "Author's Note" near the beginning of this book.)

> Be who you are
> Because the world wants to know you.
> Follow your star.
> That's the way dreams will come true.
>
> Don't try to be like everyone.
> Grow your own connection to the sun.
> Your race is only yours to run.
> Be yourself, and you'll have won.

Be who you are.
Let life's force lead and guide you.
Follow your light.
Let it show what's true for you.

Don't try to be like everyone.
Grow your own connection to the sun.
Your race is only yours to run.
Chase your bliss, and you'll have won.

Be who you are.
Let your soul's urgings move you.
Follow your heart.
It will lead you to what's true.

Don't try to be like everyone.
Grow your own connection to the sun.
Your race is only yours to run.
Live your bliss, and you'll have won.

Be who you are.
Let love's light shine through you.
Trust in yourself
Because the world wants to know you.

Be who you are.
That's the way dreams will come true.
Be who you are.
That's the way God will touch you.
Be who you are.
That's the way God lives through you.
Be who you are
Because the world wants to know you.

Kindergarten Truth

Sticks and stones may break my bones,
But words can never hurt me.
I will not succumb to moans
Because I exist beyond me.

I won't be defined by labels,
Like "nigger" and "spick" and "black" and "white".
I won't let my culture's fables
Define for me what's wrong or right.

Think of all the things you've learned.
Think of all that you've been taught.
Think of how you have been burned.
Now consider your mind's been bought.

Are you really what you see?
Are you really what you're called?
Are you really what's called "me"?
Could your reason have been mauled?

You were taught in kindergarten
That words can never hurt you,
But is that something you've forgotten,
Or was it ever really true?

Why was it considered so wise?
Why did it once feel so true?
Was it simply one of those lies
That when you're young, adults tell you?

Certainly it rings of truth.
Certainly it has deep wisdom.
Certainly it's not the folly of youth.
Certainly it leads one to freedom.

Isn't there something that comes before me,
A something that makes me possible,
A something more real than everything that's me,
A something that makes what I call "me" laughable?

What's what sees what I call "me"?
What's the thing that makes me possible?
What in me believes in being free?
What in me brings forth the impossible?

Something nearer than my heart,
Something that exists eternally.
Beyond my senses, an unseen part
That allows me to see what it is that I see.

Simply put, it comes before me
And allows me to see everything I see.
It's the spark of existence that lives within me,
And it's far beyond all that I call "me".

So take a look into the mirror; what do you see –
A honky, a coon, a faggot, a Jew?
If so, don't complain about racists; don't say, "Poor me."
Be completely honest with yourself; the "racist" is you!

Remember what we all learned in kindergarten:
"Sticks and stones may break my bones, but words can never hurt me."
Don't allow this wisdom to ever be forgotten:
I EXIST BEYOND ME.

Love Alone

You're trading your whole life for this, it said,
Some steady voice inside my head.
And what you do is what it's worth.
Your dreams will be returned to earth
Regardless of the things you choose
Or things you gain or things you lose.
For death will take it all away,
And you'll be nothing soon one day.

It's hard to live too carefully.
Fulfilling needs can feel petty
With this strange voice inside my head
Reminding me that I'll be dead.
It makes it all seem fake, a lie.
Why should I care? Why should I try
When death will take it all away,
And I'll be nothing soon one day?

Try to look past what you see,
It says. *Don't live life so narrowly.*
Life and death serve to remind
Of something else that you must find:
A deeper, richer, silent base,
Where life and death don't have a place.
And when you learn to live from there,
Alive or dead, why should you care?

It feels I walk this earth in dreams.
My bones are fragile, so it seems.
But there's a force that flows through me,
In bones and dreams, forever free.
It's really not much price to pay
That death will take it all away –
All the pain and lies and gray –
For love to stand alone one day.

Heaven Is a Place I Know

Heaven is a place I know.
It's not a place where we can go
To rest in peace after we die
Since death is just a big fat lie.
A lie meant to keep us in hell,
Inside a torturous mental shell
That limits us and makes us small,
Afraid to fly for fear we'll fall.

Heaven is a place I know.
It's not a place where I will go
If I've been good living this life
Of pain and hurt and fear and strife.
To live there I must simply know
That there's no place I need to go.
That what we live are simply dreams
In which what's real's not what it seems.

Heaven is a place I know.
It's not a place I need to go
To sense and feel and hear and see
That what makes you also makes me.
It's simply something that I feel
That makes God's love so boldly real
And transforms horrors of this place
And overrides any disgrace.

Heaven is a place I know
In which God's love moves me to grow
Beyond my needs and wants and fear
To see beyond the pain that's here.
And here's a secret I will share:
Hell is great because from there,
While you're thinking God is mean,
The best views of heaven are seen.

Heaven is a place I know
Where flowers from lifeless ground grow.
Where commendations of God's Son
Grow from His own crucifixion.
Where faith can build a bridge across
Pain and tears and death and loss.
Where gratitude overcomes hurt
To raise our spirits from the dirt.

But where is it? Well, it's right here
Beyond your ego and your fear!
And when you believe and let go,
Your faith will guide, and life will flow
In ways you'll see will clearly show
Heaven is a place you know.
Trust your heart and you will see,
Beyond your fear, beyond your "me",
Your life will into heaven grow.
Yes, heaven is a place we know.

No Truer Words Were Ever Spoken

The heart is an egg, and it's meant to be broken.
No greater truth has ever been spoken.
Tragedy makes the shell weaker and worn
To allow what's inside of our hearts to be born.

"But what is born?" you might ask.
Well, what's beneath and beyond our mask.
"But what's our mask?" you will plea.
Well, it's our ego, which lives fearfully.

The ego wants and needs and fears.
It gives us a voice to express our cheers.
But what it wants is never enough.
What can't kill fear is worthless stuff.

And so we settle for living with fear,
But that can't make us happy here.
Then our hearts lead us on with a specific notion:
A deeper yearning for a fulfilling devotion.

So we allow our hearts to lead us on
In the hopes that our empty feeling will be gone.
But we don't know that our hearts are made for breaking,
So that what's inside of them can start its waking.

Expectations not coming through
Can make us feel deeply sad and blue.
And once we feel our lives falling apart,
That makes way for a broken heart.

When we feel everything coming to an end –
All the pleasure and all the winning –
We'll realize it's not something we ourselves can mend,
And that will be a new beginning!

Then we'll cry out for *HELP* and say,
"*H*ello *E*ternal *L*oving *P*resence.
Please show me the way."
And we'll humbly surrender to God's guiding essence.

After our heart breaks and our ego is dead,
We will finally feel what it means to be free.
We will no longer be living inside our head,
And what our heart birthed will taste of eternity.

This is what is meant to be,
And this is why our heart must be broken.
What we want most is to be set free.
No truer words were ever spoken.

Consider Jesus Christ and the way that He died.
This is the GREAT TRUTH Jesus knew very well.
Jesus rose to Heaven only after being crucified.
You see, THE ROAD TO HEAVEN GOES THROUGH HELL.

Eternal

If you do not know how to die
   and come to life again,
You are but a lonely prisoner on this dark earth.
If you succumb to overwhelming fear and worry when
Your life's coming apart,
   then you don't know your true worth.

Death is simply an illusion.
What's born will die, and that's infernal.
But let us clarify confusion:
There is in us something eternal.

We feel it when we fall in love:
A deep, timeless fraternity.
And we feel guided from above
To pledge ourselves eternally.

"But what's eternal?" you might ask,
As we wallow in stupidity.
What's born is nothing but a mask.
Beyond it lies eternity.

Most religions allude to this:
That after all this pain and strife,
There's something that will feel like bliss.
A thing that's called an afterlife.

When we become tired of living from ego,
In vanity and fear and selfishness,
Growing beyond simply surviving will show
That we are eternal beingness.

And when we grow tired of just living to survive,
Of living in a torturous survival mode,
We will grow into being eternally alive
And live in a joyous eternal abode.

It's not about falling in love with life,
Simply with touching and hearing and seeing…
It's about growing beyond fear and strife…
And falling in love with our eternal being.

If you do not know how to live from beyond your ego
    and in every moment be born again,
You are but a lonely prisoner on this dark earth.
If you succumb to overwhelming fear and worry when
Your world appears to be falling apart,
    then you don't know your eternal worth.

Worse than Death

Curiosity killed the cat.
I really don't know much about that,
But what I really know is this:
Curiosity's something we shouldn't dismiss.
And this I know purely from reasoning:
A lack of curiosity can destroy a human being.

Let me try to explain it without complication.
Think very clearly about our life situation.
Consciousness requires breaks called "sleep".
To drink of the peace that from sleep we reap,
We must disconnect from consciousness
And no longer experience conscious awareness.
However, conscious awareness is just a dream
Because as profoundly real as it may seem,
It is not something that we can maintain,
Even with great effort, even if we strain.
To keep it going without sleep breaks
Is impossible and clearly demonstrates
That our conscious lives are not quite real,
And what's called "reality" is just a "raw deal".

But that should be something to rejoice
Because it leaves us with this great choice:
Do we continue believing in a lie
That tells us that one day we will die,
Or do we challenge common sense and upend this fact
That tells us we are mortal and makes us afraid to act?

Well, they say curiosity killed the cat,
But I know something far worse than that:
Lack of curiosity is an abandoning of reasoning,
And a lack of curiosity can destroy a human being.
Because to believe that you die and that you take a last breath
Is to live a life that is worse than death.

By and By

I know these arms belong to you.
These eyes, these legs... Yes, they do too.
I know these breaths I ride are yours;
Back into you all this blood pours.
I know that time's your gift to me:
To know through years all I must be,
And dance and play within your bones
In ways reflecting my own tones.

I know my home is far from here:
Beyond your needs, beyond your fear.
I know it's not an age or place
I must traverse to sense my grace.
I give back what is yours to you.
You do those lovely things you do:
To say what does not fit in words
Through ocean waves and songs of birds;
To paint what eyes could never see
Through rock and stream and sky and tree;
To do what God could never do –
Give God small feet of me and you.

I will return to this blessed place
Where love takes on a form and face:
Where flower carpets drape the ground;
Where free winds fill the air with sound;
Where fish roam oceans filled from tears,
And God's grace dresses human fears.
I will return here by and by,
Where rocks breed flesh and mountains cry.

Falling (Reprise)

Even if I sailed the sky
Across the universe and all,
Something in me would ask why
I should fear if I should fall.
Wasn't I a child of God?
Wasn't I a part of all?
Weren't my freedoms vastly broad
And just as infinitely tall?

Moving through this wondrous world
In fear is something I resent,
As if in glory I'd been hurled
Only to taste of joy half spent.
God in all God's wisdom would
Have me suffer all this pain
To learn to see the bad from good
And reap from that some earthly gain?
So then I'd sail across the sky,
But still I'd hear in me the call
To take instead the path past why
And give up fear in trade for all.

To hell with good and bad and sky.
To hell with fear and gain and all.
To hell with living wondering why
I couldn't just have faith and fall.
Wasn't I a child of God?
Wasn't I a part of all?
Isn't love so vastly broad
That it will catch me as I fall?

Have No Fear! Death Only
Happens to Other People

In the 1400s, before Christopher Columbus discovered the New World (the Western Hemisphere, which includes North and South America) in 1492, most people believed that the world was flat. Of course, there were many people, like the ancient Greeks and astronomers of that time like Galileo and Copernicus, who believed that the world was round. But it was not until the discovery of the New World that the belief the world is round began to become the common belief.

Do you ever wonder what in our current common beliefs could be as ridiculous as believing that the world is flat? I do, and this is what it is: that we die, that our existence is flat and has ends like a flat world. Of course, there are many people, like Jesus Christ and people who have had near-death experiences, who tell us that there is life – that we continue to exist – after death. But do we really believe that? If so, if we truly believe that we will continue to exist after we "die", then why are we so worried about surviving? And more specifically, why do we fear death and, consequently, fear truly living, living without fear? Could it be that we are as ridiculous as the people who believed that the world was flat before

1492? I believe that we should have no fear because death only happens to other people. Let me explain what I mean.

Death only happens to other people. I know this sounds very strange, but instead of talking about death, let's talk about sleep first. And let's say that "Sleep only happens to other people." You see, being asleep is not really a personal experience; it is not something that we really experience. We experience feeling tired and "getting sleepy" before falling asleep, and we experience feeling refreshed and "waking up" after having been asleep. But we never experience what happens between the getting sleepy and the waking up experiences. In other words, we never truly experience "being asleep" because there is never a moment in which we can say, "I am sleeping." If we can, it's because we are dreaming, not sleeping. This moment is beyond our experience. So sleep only happens to other people because we never personally experience being asleep. We see other people asleep and apparently experiencing being asleep, but it is not a personal experience. Being asleep is an imaginary personal experience that we have created to explain what happens between the getting sleepy and the waking up authentic personal experiences. Do you follow me so far?

I propose that death is also something that, like sleep, only happens to other people. In other words, death is not a personal experience; it is only an imaginary personal experience that we have created to refer to the condition that we supposedly experienced before we were born and will supposedly experience after our physical bodies can no longer operate properly. So do we really die? Well, from the point of view of other people, yes, we die. In other words, other people will see us as dead. But from a personal point of view, no, we do not die; we do not personally experience being dead and do not cease to exist.

Now here's a big question: How would you choose to live if you knew that you do not die, that you do not cease to exist? Would you choose to live your life differently than you live your life now? Well, would you? Think about that.

Something more to think about. Life and death are two sides of the same coin, so if death is only an imaginary experience (as explained above) then isn't life, by association, also only an imaginary experience? This confirms what we all learned in kindergarten: "Row, row, row your boat, gently down the stream. Merrily, merrily, merrily, merrily, *life is but a dream.*"

So have no fear! Death only happens to other people. Let's put that on a T-shirt and make it as popular as "Just do it!" (the Nike slogan).

To serve progress and evolution, one must go beyond the status quo, beyond the usual, beyond the normal. All profound advancement redefines common sense and creates a new vision of reality and of what is possible. In this growth process, there are those who commit to the new vision to move forward, and there are those who stay married to the old vision – the old version of common sense – to stay the same. It takes courage to adopt a new version of common sense and move forward into a new vision of reality and of what is possible. And be aware that the opposite of courage is not fear; it is conformity. Be brave!

The hardest thing to see is what is in front of your eyes.
– Johann Wolfgang von Goethe

Being Blinded by Normality

When I was young, I suspected that I might actually be crazy, but I reasoned that I was not crazy because I could effectively pretend to be normal. However, I suspected that what was considered normal was completely insane, and as I grew older and became more knowledgeable my suspicion grew into a conviction and then into a conclusion – a conclusion that what we consider normal is absolutely crazy. This short chapter relates to that. It contains some interesting thoughts about being blinded by normality. Or more specifically, about limiting our vision of the world to what is considered the normal, although it may be completely inaccurate.

Can you imagine what it must have been like to live in the early 1400s and believe that the world is flat? Of course, now we look back and find it hard to believe people actually believed that the world was flat. Why did they believe that? Were they stupid? Were they crazy? Well, let me show you how it felt to be "stupid" or "crazy" in the early 1400s, before Christopher Columbus discovered the New World.

Just like you can look into the sky and see that the moon and sun are round and conclude that the Earth is also round, there are simple things that we can see in our lives to help us conclude that we are eternal (that we are not mortal — that we do not die. That we actually live eternally). For example, there are many cases of people who die — who are pronounced dead by science — in hospital operating rooms and are then brought back to life. These people have interesting stories to share about their experiences, which are called "near-death experiences". So like looking into the sky and seeing that the moon and sun are round and using this information to conclude that the Earth is also round, these near-death experiences can be used to conclude that we do not die, that we are eternal.

Now I give you another example of how it felt to be "stupid" or "crazy" in the early 1400s, before Christopher Columbus discovered the New World.

Conscious existence is not as real as it appears to be. Consider this. When you watch a movie, you know that the movie is not real, although you might react to the movie emotionally (for example, you might cry) as if what you are seeing in the movie is really happening. You know it's not real because the movie ends, you leave the movie theater, and continue living your real life. So there is the movie reality, which is not real because it ends and for many other reasons, and there is the life outside the movie theater reality, which we consider the true reality, or at least more real than the movie reality. However, it is also not continuous. It ends every day when we grow too tired to continue operating in conscious existence, and supposedly, it ends when we die. However, like I said, conscious existence is not as real as it appears to be, and the fact that it is not continuous is a big clue to that fact. Just like the fact that the moon and sun are round are big clues that the Earth is also round, it is very easy to see that conscious existence is not real because, like a movie, it ends. So if what we experience outside a movie theater, what we call "life", is more real than what we experience inside a movie theater, which we call "a movie", what is more real than conscious existence? Well, just like so-called real life happens outside a movie theater, what happens outside conscious existence is what we experience when we are asleep because sleep is the thing that regularly interrupts conscious existence and does not allow it to be continuous. But what do we experience when we are asleep? It is something beyond our thoughts and conscious existence, which is composed of thoughts. However, because it is the larger reality within which the "reality" of our conscious existence takes place, couldn't you say that it is actually more real than our conscious existence, which is just an imagined reality (an experience that we imagine to be real) that occurs within this larger reality we call "being asleep", just like the movie reality occurs within the larger reality that occurs outside the movie theater?

Now you know why I say that conscious existence is not as real as it appears to be. But so what? The purpose of this brief text is not to convince you that conscious existence is an artificial reality that occurs within a larger reality we experience when we are asleep. That is a subject matter that deserves a whole book to explore. The purpose of this brief text is simply to show you how it feels to be blinded by normality, and more specifically, to show you how it felt to be "stupid" or "crazy" in the early 1400s, before Christopher Columbus discovered the New World. So how does it feel? Of course, it feels normal because almost everybody would not be able to see the logic of this explanation because they are blinded by normality, just like almost everybody was blinded by normality in the early 1400s and could not see the logic of seeing that the moon and sun were round and using that information to conclude that the Earth is also round. But you might say, "Well then, normal is stupid." I would not disagree with that. But the funny thing is that stupidity has a lot of company because most people would rather think like the majority of people than to think differently and feel alone. So would you rather be blinded by normality and be stupid but part of the large group called "most people", or would you rather think outside the box and live using the complete power of your reasoning ability?

I prefer to use the complete power of my reasoning ability. Anyway, now you know what it felt like to be stupid or crazy – to be blinded by normality – in the early 1400s. However, you don't need to feel alone if you prefer not to be blinded by normality. You can write to me (my e-mail address appears in the "Author's Note" near the beginning of this book and in the "Invitation" at the end of this book) to communicate with somebody who prefers not to be blinded by normality with respect to whether we are mortal or immortal beings. And we can start a community together consisting of individuals eager to raise the awareness that we are eternal beings, that death is a lie, and that the only thing we have to fear is fear itself, as President Franklin D. Roosevelt famously stated in 1933.

I would love to hear from you.

Invitation

Although many of my poems could be considered very spiritual, and I consider myself a rather spiritual person, I feel that we need to act on our beliefs in order to make them real. I like to tell myself that it is one thing to be able to understand something, another thing to be able to believe something, and yet another thing to be able to live something (to be able to act on your beliefs). What is most important about my poems and my spiritual ideas to me is to be able to live them, to be able to act on what they teach. To this end, I am making an effort to develop three practical projects to transform our world for the better to create what I call a World Without Walls. But I need a lot of help to develop these projects. I invite you to contact me at my primary e-mail address (dleon19@atlanticbb.net) or at my backup e-mail address (dleon1919@yahoo.com) if you would like me to send you the PDF of my book about the meaning of life (at no cost to you) so that you can read about these projects. Then you can decide whether you would like to join my efforts to develop these projects.

I feel that these three practical projects could transform the world as significantly as YouTube, PayPal, and Facebook have transformed the world. So if you are curious and think you might want to be involved in developing such impactful projects to transform our world – and possibly get rich in the process – write to me to get the PDF of my book about the meaning of life, read about these projects to transform our world for the better, and then decide whether you would like to be involved.

In this grand party we call life,
Seek the hearts of the dancing souls
For they have learned to see past strife
And make real on Earth heavenly goals.

You can also see videos about me and the World Without Walls project on YouTube. Look for "The World Without Walls" on YouTube to find my YouTube channel and see these videos.

CPSIA information can be obtained
at www.ICGtesting.com
Printed in the USA
BVHW041742220719
554056BV00017B/814/P